I AM...

*... is an inspirational, visually colorful poetic book made to uplift and empower one's higher
self-awareness to emphasize being connected to everyone and everything in the universe*

...The ENERGY & Power of "I AM" can enable you and your child to discover distinctive abilities within that can lead to a more productive life by repeating positive affirmations which will build up an individual's self-esteem and transform their sense of self

I AM= Spiritual Energy that which shall not be born nor die (omnipresent & omniscient)

Written & Created by Q. Rogers, M.Ed

No part of the publication may be reproduced in whole or part, or stored in a retrieval system, or transmitted in any form or by any mean, electronic, mechanical, photocopying, recording, or otherwise without the written permission of the publisher/author.

I AM...

For we are all made in "I AM" image and likeness

Dedicated to
To my children and my children's children

❤️

Love You Daddy!

I AM= The MOST High- Spiritual Being

WHO AM I?

WHAT AM I?

I AM...

A Miracle   Magnificent   Marvelous

Short   Tall   Big   Small   Above-Average

Upper-Class   Middle-Class   Working-Class

Girl   Boy   Woman   Man   Gender-Neutral

King   Queen   God   Goddess   Spiritual-being

Healing   Happy   LOVE   Healthy   Hopeful

Smart   Clever   Wise   Brilliant

Perfect   Unique   Complete

(I AM ONE with ALL)

I am a reflection of the "I AM"

How do I see myself?
Circle all that applies to you...

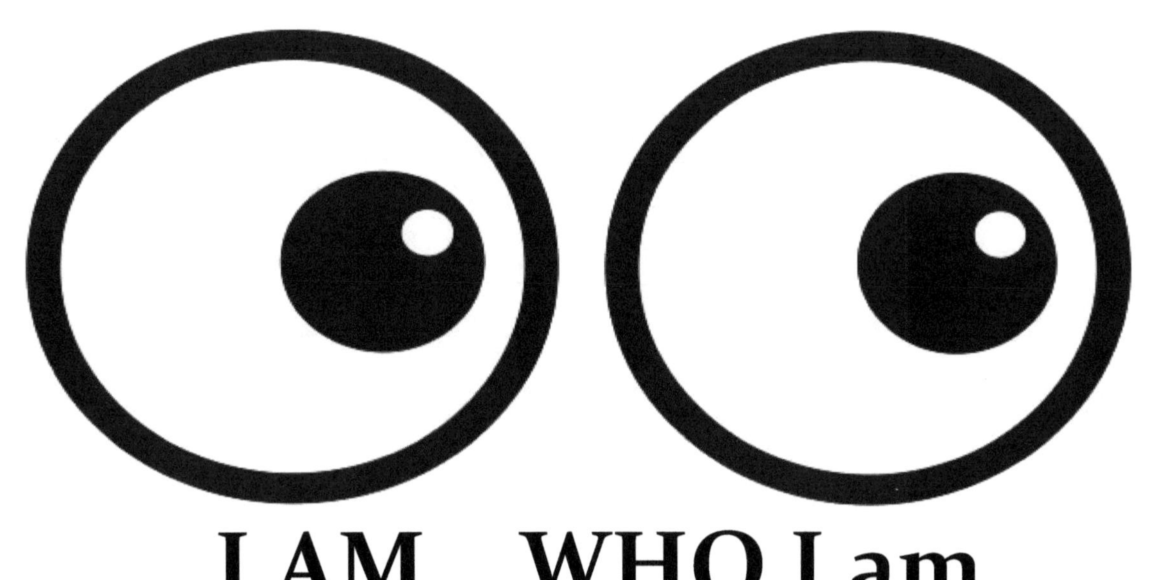

I AM... WHO I am

I AM... WHAT I am

I AM... HOW I am

I AM... WHERE I am

I AM... WHY I am

...Am I the I AM?

I AM… He/ She/It/ They/Us.

You can find me on a train, plane, car, or bus.

I AM… you. You are connected to me.

Open your heart and you will see.

I AM everywhere
at the same time.

Let's hear it again
and press rewind.

Am I… "I AM?"

Yes, I am the I AM.

Egg-cellent!

I AM.... very different

I AM.... the same

Egg-actly.... I will remain

I AM here

I AM there

I AM everywhere

I AM Winter   I AM Spring

I AM one with everything.

I AM one with all.

I AM... young.

I AM... old.

I AM... hot.   I AM... cold.

I AM... future.

I AM... past.

I AM... slow.

I AM... fast.

"I AM" in everyone and in every living thing.
Let's come together, hold hands and sing!

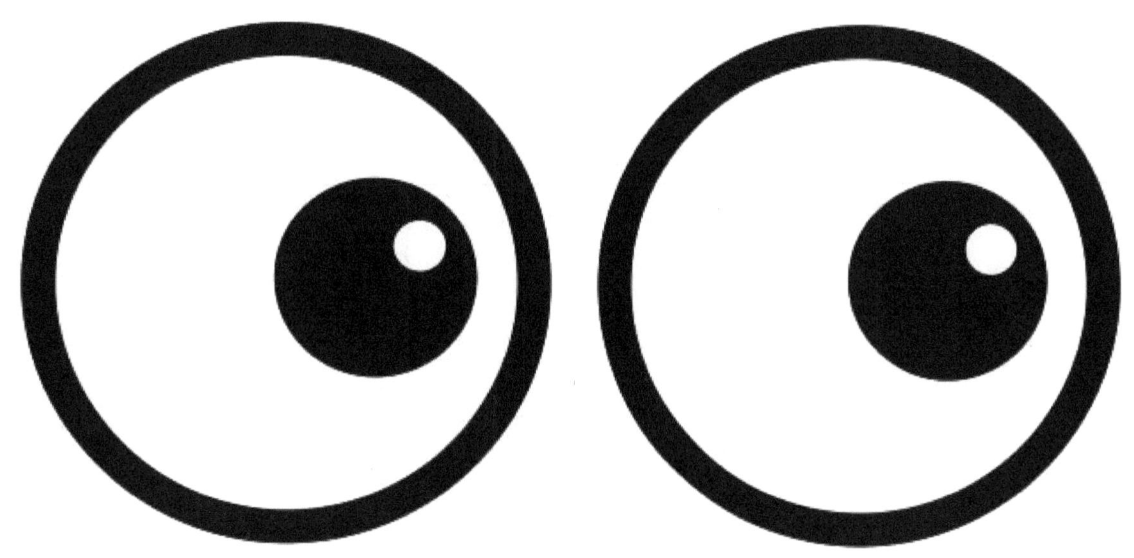

I AM... WHO I say I am

I AM... WHAT I think I am

I AM... HOW I feel I am

I AM... WHERE I know I am

I AM... WHY the way I am

...I AM the I AM

I AM Happy

I AM Handy

I AM Harmony

I AM Healthy

I AM Powerful

I AM Perfect

I AM Positive

I AM Peaceful

I AM... the beginning.
I AM... the end.
I AM the I AM
Win... Win...Win!

I AM...

...From the same Father/ Egg
(DNA-Spirit)

I AM limitless energy expressed in human form.

I was never born.
Therefore, I can never die.

Wow, no need to cry.
I AM …is not in the sky.

I AM …is always with
you and within you.

That's why… and so it is.

No matter what color we are on the outside,
we are all the same on the inside.

I AM Blessed......I Believe in Myself!

Draw a positive picture of yourself…